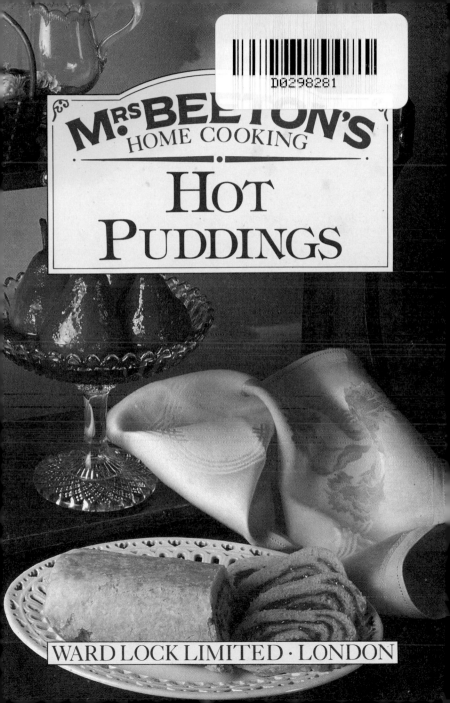

Mrs BEETON'S
HOME COOKING

HOT
PUDDINGS

WARD LOCK LIMITED · LONDON

© Ward Lock Limited 1986

First published in Great Britain in 1986 by Ward Lock Limited, 8 Clifford Street, London W1X 1RB, an Egmont Company.

Edited by Susan Dixon
Designed by Melissa Orrom
Text filmset in Caslon 540
by Cheney & Sons Limited
Printed and bound in Italy
by L.E.G.O.

British Library Cataloguing in Publication Data

Hot puddings.—
(Mrs. Beeton home cooking)
  1. Desserts
  I. Title II. series
  641.8'6   TX773

ISBN 0-7063-6458-9

Notes

The recipes in this book have been tested in metric weights and measures. These have been based on equivalents of 25g to 1 oz, 500g to 1 lb and 500ml to 1 pint, with some adjustments where necessary.

It is important to follow *either* the metric *or* the imperial measures. Do not use a combination of measures.

HOT PUDDINGS

For dishing a boiled pudding as soon as it comes out of the pot, dip it into a basin of cold water, and the cloth will then not adhere to it. Great expedition is necessary in sending puddings to table, as, by standing, they quickly become heavy, batter puddings particularly.

Isabella Beeton 1861

On pages 2 and 3
From the top, clockwise
Tapioca Cream Pudding (page 13), Pears in Wine (page 56) and
Roly-Poly Pudding (page 32)

MILK PUDDINGS

CARAMEL RICE PUDDING

6 helpings

125g/5oz Carolina *or* similar rice
750ml/1½ pints milk
a pinch of salt
75g/3oz lump sugar

75ml/3fl oz water
2 eggs
40g/1½oz caster sugar

Wash the rice, and put it into a saucepan with the milk and salt. Bring to simmering point and simmer for about 1 hour or until the rice is soft and all the milk has been absorbed.

Meanwhile, prepare a thickly folded band of newspaper long enough to encircle a 1 litre/2 pint charlotte mould (it can then be held firmly in one hand when heated). Heat the mould in boiling water or in the oven and wrap the newspaper round it. Prepare the caramel by heating the sugar and water together, stirring until it boils. Remove the spoon and leave it to boil, without stirring, until golden-brown. Immediately, pour the caramel into the warmed charlotte mould; twist and turn it until the sides and base are evenly coated. Leave to harden for a few minutes.

Beat the eggs until liquid and stir them into the cooked rice with the sugar. Turn into the prepared mould, cover with greased greaseproof paper or foil, and steam for 1 hour or until firm. Turn out, if liked. Serve hot or cold.

Caramel Rice Pudding

LEMON RICE

6 helpings

50g/2oz Carolina *or* similar rice
500ml/1 pint milk
a pinch of salt
pared rind and juice of 1 lemon
75g/3oz granulated sugar
2 eggs

butter for greasing
3×15ml spoons/3 tablespoons
   smooth seedless jam
50g/2oz caster sugar
caster sugar for dredging

Wash the rice and put it in a double boiler with the milk, salt, and lemon rind; simmer for about 1 hour or until tender. Remove the rind and stir in the granulated sugar. Cool slightly. Separate the eggs. Stir the yolks and lemon juice into the rice. Pour into a buttered 1 litre/2 pint dish and bake in a warm oven at 160°C/325°F/Gas 3, for 20–25 minutes. Spread the jam on top of the pudding. Whisk the egg whites until stiff, and fold in the caster sugar. Pile on top of the pudding, dredge with a little extra caster sugar, and bake in a very cool oven at 140°C/275°F/Gas 1, for 20–30 minutes until the meringue is set and coloured.

WINDSOR PUDDING

— *6 helpings* —

40g/1½oz Carolina *or* similar rice
375ml/¾ pint milk
1kg/2lb cooking apples

grated *or* pared rind and juice of ½
    lemon (see Method)
50g/2oz caster sugar
3 eggs
butter for greasing

Wash the rice and simmer it in the milk for 45 minutes – 1 hour or until the rice is tender and all the milk has been absorbed. Cool slightly. Peel, core, and chop the apples roughly, and stew in a covered pan until soft. Shake the pan from time to time to prevent them sticking. Rub the apples through a sieve, then add the grated rind and juice of the lemon. Alternatively, process the apples in an electric blender with the pared rind and juice. Stir the cooked rice into the apples with the sugar. Separate the eggs; whisk the whites until fairly stiff and fold them into the mixture. Put the mixture into a buttered 1 litre/2 pint basin, cover with greased greaseproof paper or foil, and steam very gently for 40–45 minutes.

Serve with Pouring Custard (page 17).

EARS OF RICE.

HOT TIMBALE OF SEMOLINA

6 helpings

butter for greasing
500ml/1 pint milk
75g/3oz semolina
50g/2oz caster sugar

a few drops vanilla essence
2 eggs
2×15ml spoons/2 tablespoons
    single cream

DECORATION

6 canned apricot halves
250ml/½ pint apricot syrup from
    can
1 strip angelica

3 glacé cherries
1×10ml spoon/1 dessertspoon
    chopped almonds

Butter a 750ml/1½ pint timbale mould or 8 small dariole moulds. Heat the milk, sprinkle in the semolina, stirring all the time, and simmer for 10–15 minutes until it is cooked. Cool slightly. Add the sugar and vanilla essence. Separate the eggs, and stir the yolks into the mixture. Beat with an electric or rotary whisk until it is nearly cold. Whisk the egg whites until just stiff, and fold into the mixture with the cream. Three-quarters fill the timbale mould or small moulds with the mixture. Cover with greased greaseproof paper or foil. Steam a large mould for about 45 minutes and small moulds for 30 minutes or until set.

Meanwhile, heat the apricots between 2 plates over simmering water. Boil the apricot syrup until well reduced. When the pudding is cooked and set, turn out on to a hot dish and decorate with halved apricots, angelica, glacé cherries and chopped almonds. Pour the syrup round and serve.

Hot Timbale of Semolina

HONEY PUDDING

125ml/¼ pint milk
25g/1oz semolina
2 eggs
25g/1oz butter
100g/4oz honey

grated rind of ½ lemon
1×2.5ml spoon/½ teaspoon
　ground ginger
150g/5oz stale white breadcrumbs
fat for greasing

Heat the milk, sprinkle in the semolina, and cook for 10 minutes, stirring all the time. Separate the eggs. Add the yolks to the semolina with the butter, honey, lemon rind, ground ginger, and breadcrumbs. Beat well. Whisk the egg whites until fairly stiff and fold into the mixture. Put into a greased 625–750ml/1¼–1½ pint basin, cover with greased greaseproof paper or foil, and steam gently for 1¾–2 hours.

TAPIOCA CREAM PUDDING

75g/3oz tapioca
750ml/1½ pints milk
a pinch of salt
15g/½oz butter *or* margarine
1×15ml spoon/1 tablespoon caster
  sugar

½×2.5ml spoon/¼ teaspoon
  almond essence
3 eggs
butter for greasing
75g/3oz ratafias *or* small macaroons

Wash the tapioca and soak in the milk for 1–2 hours with the salt. Heat to simmering point, and simmer for about 1 hour until the grain is soft and all the milk has been absorbed. Add the butter, sugar, and essence. Cool slightly. Separate the eggs and stir the yolks into the tapioca. Pour the mixture into a buttered 1 litre/2 pint pie dish, and bake in a moderate oven at 180°C/350°F/Gas 4, for 15–20 minutes. Crush the ratafias or macaroons. Whisk the egg whites until stiff and fold in the biscuits. Pile on top of the tapioca. Bake in a very cool oven at 140°C/275°F/Gas 1, for 20–30 minutes.

MACAROONS.

SOURED MILK PANCAKES

100g/4oz plain flour
a pinch of salt
1 egg
125ml/¼ pint soured milk
1×10ml spoon/1 dessertspoon
   melted butter

½×2.5ml spoon/¼ teaspoon
   bicarbonate of soda
1×10ml spoon/1 dessertspoon hot
   water
fat *or* oil for frying
caster sugar

FILLING

250ml/½ pint mashed sweetened
   ripe fruit (see **Note**)

Sift the flour and salt into a bowl, make a well in the centre, and add the egg. Stir in the milk, gradually working the flour down from the sides. Beat vigorously until the mixture is smooth and bubbly. Add the butter. Dissolve the bicarbonate of soda in the hot water and stir into the mixture. Pour the batter into a jug. Heat a little fat or oil in a frying pan, and pour off any excess. Pour a little batter into the pan to make a pancake about 7.5cm/3 inches in diameter. As soon as it rises and is brown underneath, but before the bubbles break, turn the pancake over and fry the other side until golden-brown. Keep each cooked pancake warm in a tea-towel. Cook the rest of the batter in the same way, greasing the pan when necessary. The cooked pancakes will be thick and fluffy.

For each person, sandwich 3 pancakes together with the fruit. Sprinkle with caster sugar.

Note Use any soft fruit except currants, eg skinned, stoned peaches, apricots or plums, or well-drained stewed fruit or crushed pineapple.

Soured Milk Pancakes

QUEEN OF PUDDINGS

4 helpings

75g/3oz soft white breadcrumbs
400ml/16fl oz milk
25g/1oz butter
2×5ml spoons/2 teaspoons grated
   lemon rind

2 eggs
75g/3oz caster sugar
fat for greasing
2×15ml spoons/2 tablespoons red
   jam

Dry the breadcrumbs slightly by placing in a cool oven for a few moments. Warm the milk with the butter and lemon rind, to approximately 65°C/149°F; do not let it come near the boil. Separate the eggs and stir 25g/1oz of the sugar into the yolks. Pour the warmed milk over the yolks, and stir in well. Add the crumbs and mix thoroughly. Pour the custard mixture into a greased 750ml/1½ pint pie dish and leave to stand for 30 minutes. Bake in a warm oven at 160°C/325°F/Gas 3, for 40–45 minutes until the pudding is lightly set.

Remove the pudding from the oven and reduce the temperature to 120°C/250°F/Gas ½. Warm the jam and spread it over the pudding. Whisk the egg whites until stiff, add half the remaining sugar and whisk again. Fold in nearly all the remaining sugar. Spoon the meringue round the edge of the jam and sprinkle with the remainder of the caster sugar. (The piled-up meringue and the red jam centre then suggest a crown.) Return the pudding to the oven for 40–45 minutes or until the meringue is set.

CRÈME BRÛLÉE

---
4 helpings

1×15ml spoon/1 tablespoon
   cornflour
250ml/½ pint milk
250ml/½ pint cream
a few drops vanilla essence

3 eggs
50g/2oz caster sugar
fat for greasing
ground cinnamon (optional)

Blend the cornflour to a smooth paste with a little of the milk, and bring the rest of the milk to the boil. Pour the boiling milk on to the blended cornflour, stirring well. Return the mixture to the pan, bring to the boil and boil for 1 minute, stirring all the time. Remove from the heat and leave to cool. Beat together the cream, vanilla essence, and eggs. Stir into the cooled mixture. Whisk over low heat for about 30 minutes or until the custard thickens; do not boil. Add 25g/1oz sugar and pour into a greased 625ml/1¼ pint flameproof dish. Sprinkle the pudding with the rest of the sugar and a little cinnamon, if used. Place under a hot grill for 10 minutes or until the sugar has melted and turned brown. Keep the custard about 10cm/4 inches from the heat. Serve hot or cold.

Alternatively, bake in a fairly hot oven at 200°C/400°F/Gas 6, for about 15 minutes until the pudding is browned.

BREAD AND BUTTER PUDDING

4 helpings

butter for greasing
4 thin slices bread (100g/4oz
    approx)
25g/1oz butter
50g/2oz sultanas *or* currants

a pinch of nutmeg *or* cinnamon
400ml/16fl oz milk
2 eggs
25g/1oz granulated sugar

Grease a 1 litre/2 pint pie dish. Cut the crusts off the bread and spread the slices with the butter. Cut the bread into squares or triangles and arrange in alternate layers, buttered side up, with the sultanas or currants. Sprinkle each layer lightly with spice. Arrange the top layer of bread in an attractive pattern. Warm the milk to approximately 65°C/149°F; do not let it come near the boil. Beat together the eggs and most of the sugar with a fork and stir in the milk. Strain the custard over the bread, sprinkle some nutmeg and the remaining sugar on top, and leave to stand for 30 minutes. Bake in a moderate oven at 180°C/350°F/Gas 4, for 30–40 minutes until set and lightly browned.

Bread and Butter Pudding

WINTER PUDDING

4 helpings

500g/1lb cooking apples
75g/3oz cooking dates
75g/3oz seedless raisins
25g/1oz cut mixed peel
1×5ml spoon/1 teaspoon grated
   nutmeg

2 pieces plain cake *or* trifle sponges
   (5×7.5cm/2×3 inches approx)
2 eggs
300ml/12fl oz milk
fat for greasing

Peel, core, and slice the apples. Chop the dates. Put with the raisins, peel, nutmeg, and a little water into a saucepan, cover, and simmer gently until tender. Crumble the cake finely. Beat the eggs lightly with a fork and stir in the milk. Add the crumbs, stir, and leave to stand for 10 minutes. Drain the stewed fruit, put it into a greased 750ml/1½ pint pie dish and level the top. Pour the custard mixture over the fruit. Bake in a warm oven at 160°C/325°F/Gas 3, for 1–1¼ hours until the top of the pudding is browned.

Serve with cream.

LEMON DELICIOUS PUDDING

4 helpings

3 eggs
1×15ml spoon/1 tablespoon
  self-raising flour
75g/3oz caster sugar
200ml/8fl oz milk
juice and grated rind of 2 large
  lemons

a pinch of salt
1×15ml spoon/1 tablespoon icing
  sugar
butter for greasing

Separate the eggs, Sift the flour. Beat the yolks with the caster sugar until light, pale and creamy. Whisk the milk, flour, lemon juice, and rind into the egg yolks. Whisk the egg whites with the salt, adding the icing sugar gradually. Continue to whisk until stiff but not dry. Fold into the lemon mixture. Grease a deep 1 litre/2 pint ovenproof dish and pour the mixture into it. Stand the dish in a shallow pan of cold water and bake in a moderate oven at 180°C/350°F/Gas 4, for 1 hour.

Note This pudding has a light spongy top with lemon sauce underneath.

THE LEMON.

CABINET PUDDING

50g/2oz glacé cherries *or* seedless
   raisins
2×15ml spoons/2 tablespoons
   medium-sweet sherry
fat for greasing
4 individual trifle sponges
   (5×7.5cm/2×3 inches approx)

9 ratafias *or* 2 macaroons
400ml/16fl oz milk
3 eggs
25g/1oz caster sugar
a few drops vanilla essence

DECORATION

glacé cherries

angelica

Soak the glacé cherries or raisins in the sherry. Grease a 12.5cm/5 inch round cake tin and line the base with oiled greaseproof paper. Cut up the cherries and angelica for the decoration. Decorate the bottom of the tin with them. Cut the sponges into 1.25cm/½ inch dice, crumble the ratafias or macaroons and mix them together. Drain the dried fruit. Put alternate layers of cake and fruit in the tin. Warm the milk to approximately 65°C/149°F; do not let it come near the boil. Beat the eggs and sugar together with a fork and stir in the milk. Add a few drops of vanilla essence. Strain the custard into the tin slowly, so as not to disturb the decoration. Leave to stand for 1 hour. Cover with greased foil or greaseproof paper and steam gently for 1 hour. Remove the pudding from the steamer, leave to stand for a few minutes, turn out on to a warmed dish and peel off the paper.

ORANGE CUSTARD

pared rind and juice of 3 oranges
50g/2oz caster sugar

375ml/¾ pint boiling water
4 eggs

Put the orange rind, sugar, and boiling water into a basin, cover and leave for 2 hours. Strain the liquid into a pan, and warm but do not boil it. Beat the eggs together and stir in the liquid. Strain the custard into the pan and heat very gently, stirring all the time with a wooden spoon until the custard thickens. Do not boil or the mixture will curdle. Strain the orange juice into the custard, and stir. Pour into 4 glasses and serve warm or chilled, topped with cream.

BAKED SOUFFLÉ OMELET

2 helpings

fat for greasing
4×15ml spoons/4 tablespoons jam
  or stewed fruit
4 eggs
50g/2oz caster sugar

2×15ml spoons/2 tablespoons
  water
a pinch of salt
caster *or* icing sugar for dredging

Heat the oven to fairly hot, 190°C/375°F/Gas 5. Grease a shallow 22.5cm/9 inch ovenproof dish and spread the jam or fruit over the base. Separate the eggs. Beat the yolks with the sugar and add the water. Whisk the egg whites and salt until stiff and fold into the yolk mixture. Pour over the jam or fruit and bake for 15–20 minutes. Dredge with sugar, and serve at once.

FLOATING ISLANDS

3 eggs
200g/7oz caster sugar

500ml/1 pint milk
a few drops vanilla essence

Separate the eggs. Whisk the egg whites until very stiff. Fold in 150g/5oz caster sugar. Pour the milk into a frying pan and add a few drops of vanilla essence. Heat gently until the surface of the milk is just shivering. It must not boil or the milk will discolour and form a skin. Using 2 dessertspoons, mould egg shapes from the meringue and slide them into the milk. Make only a few at a time, and leave plenty of space between them in the pan as they swell when cooking. Cook slowly for 5 minutes, then turn them over, using a palette knife and a spoon, and cook for a further 5 minutes. They are very delicate and must be handled with care. Remove from the milk gently and place on a cloth or soft kitchen paper to drain. Continue making shapes from the meringue and poaching them in milk, until all the meringue is used. Arrange the 'islands' in a flat serving dish.

Blend the egg yolks with the rest of the sugar, then stir in the milk gently, stirring all the time, until the sauce thickens slightly. Do not let it come near the boil or it will curdle. Pour the custard round the 'islands' and serve at once.

BOILED & STEAMED PUDDINGS

GOLDEN SYRUP PUDDING

6–7 helpings

fat for greasing
3×15ml spoons/3 tablespoons
   golden syrup
150g/5oz plain flour
1×5ml spoon/1 teaspoon
   bicarbonate of soda
a pinch of salt
1×5ml spoon/1 teaspoon ground
   ginger

150g/5oz stale white breadcrumbs
100g/4oz shredded suet
50g/2oz caster sugar
1 egg
1×15ml spoon/1 tablespoon black
   treacle
75–100ml/3–4fl oz milk

Grease a 1 litre/2 pint basin, and put 1×15ml spoon/1 tablespoon of golden syrup in the bottom. Sift together the flour, bicarbonate of soda, salt, and ginger. Add the breadcrumbs, suet, and sugar. Beat together the egg, remaining syrup, treacle, and 75ml/3fl oz of the milk. Stir this mixture into the dry ingredients, adding more milk if required, to make a soft dropping consistency. Put into the basin, cover with greased paper or foil and steam for 1½–2 hours. Leave for 5–10 minutes to firm up, then turn out.

Serve with warmed golden syrup and whipped cream.

Golden Syrup Pudding

ROLY-POLY PUDDING

6–7 helpings

300g/10oz plain flour
½×2.5ml spoon/¼ teaspoon salt
2×5ml spoons/2 teaspoons baking
   powder

150g/5oz shredded suet
cold water
flour for dusting
jam for spreading

Sift the flour, salt, and baking powder together. Add the suet, and enough cold water to make a soft but not sticky dough. Roll out into a rectangle about 6mm/¼ inch thick, and spread with jam almost to the edge. Dampen the edges and roll up lightly. Seal the edges. Lay the dough on a scalded, well-floured pudding cloth and tie up the ends of the cloth. Put into a saucepan of fast-boiling water, reduce the heat and simmer for 2–2½ hours. Drain well and unwrap.

Serve sliced, with any sweet sauce.

RAISIN-GRAPE.

CHRISTMAS PUDDING

6 helpings per pudding

fat for greasing
200g/7oz plain flour
a pinch of salt
1×5ml spoon/1 teaspoon ground
   ginger
1×5ml spoon/1 teaspoon mixed
   spice
1×5ml spoon/1 teaspoon grated
   nutmeg
50g/2oz chopped blanched
   almonds
400g/13oz light *or* dark brown sugar

250g/8oz shredded suet
250g/8oz sultanas
250g/8oz currants
200g/7oz seedless raisins
200g/7oz cut mixed peel
175g/6oz stale white breadcrumbs
6 eggs
75ml/3fl oz stout
juice of 1 orange
50ml/2fl oz brandy *or* to taste
125–250ml/¼–½ pint milk

Grease four 625ml/1¼ pint basins, Sift together the flour, salt, ginger, mixed spice, and nutmeg into a mixing bowl. Add the nuts, sugar, suet, sultanas, currants, raisins, peel, and breadcrumbs. Beat together the eggs, stout, orange juice, brandy, and 125ml/¼ pint milk. Stir this into the dry ingredients, adding more milk if required, to give a soft dropping consistency. Put the mixture into the prepared basins, cover with greased paper or foil, and a floured cloth. Put into deep boiling water and boil steadily for 6–7 hours, or half steam for the same length of time.

To store, cover with a clean dry cloth, wrap in greaseproof paper and store in a cool place until required. To re-heat, boil or steam for 1½–2 hours. Serve with Pouring Custard (page 17).

CLOUTIE DUMPLING

50g/2oz muscatel raisins
125g/5oz shredded suet
300g/10oz self-raising flour
125g/5oz soft light brown sugar
125g/5oz sultanas
1×5ml spoon/1 teaspoon baking
    powder
1×5ml spoon/1 teaspoon mixed
    spice
1×5ml spoon/1 teaspoon ground
    ginger

1×5ml spoon/1 teaspoon ground
    cinnamon
50g/2oz cut mixed peel
1×2.5ml spoon/½ teaspoon salt
1 medium sized carrot (100g/4oz
    approx) *or* eating apple
125g/5oz black treacle
200ml/8fl oz milk
1 egg
flour for dusting *or* fat for greasing

De-seed the raisins. Mix the suet, dry ingredients and dried fruit together in a large bowl. Peel the apple if used. Grate the carrot or apple, and add to the dry ingredients. Dissolve the treacle in the milk over low heat. Mix into the dry ingredients to make a fairly soft dropping consistency. Mix in the egg, blending thoroughly.

Put the mixture into a scalded floured cloth, tie with string, allowing room for expansion. Place on a plate in a saucepan and fill up with water to three-quarters of the way up the dumpling. Simmer for 3 hours. Alternatively, steam the dumpling in a 1.5 litre/3 pint greased basin covered with greased paper or foil.

Serve hot or cold with a custard (page 17).

Cloutie Dumpling

MRS BEETON'S BACHELOR'S PUDDING

—————— 5–6 helpings ——————

150g/5oz cooking apples
100g/4oz stale white breadcrumbs
grated rind of ½ lemon
100g/4oz currants
75g/3oz caster sugar
a pinch of salt

½×2.5ml spoon/¼ teaspoon
   grated nutmeg
2 eggs
milk
1×5ml spoon/1 teaspoon baking
   powder
fat for greasing

Peel, core, and chop the apples coarsely. Mix together the breadcrumbs, apples, grated lemon rind, currants, sugar, salt and nutmeg. Beat the eggs until liquid and add to the dry ingredients with enough milk to form a soft dropping consistency. Leave to stand for 30 minutes. Stir in the baking powder. Put the mixture into a greased 1 litre/2 pint basin, cover with greased paper or foil and steam for 2½–3 hours. Leave in the basin for a few minutes, then turn out.

CHOCOLATE PUDDING

5–6 helpings

fat for greasing
50g/2oz plain chocolate
125ml/¼ pint milk
40g/1½oz butter *or* margarine
40g/1½oz sugar

2 eggs
100g/4oz stale white breadcrumbs
½×2.5ml spoon/¼ teaspoon
  baking powder

Grease a 750ml/1½ pint basin or 6 dariole moulds. Grate the chocolate into a saucepan, add the milk and heat slowly to dissolve the chocolate. Cream together the fat and sugar. Separate the eggs and beat the yolks into the creamed mixture. Add the melted chocolate, breadcrumbs, and baking powder. Whisk the egg whites until fairly stiff and fold into the mixture. Put into the basin or moulds, cover with greased paper or foil, and steam for 1 hour for a large pudding, and 30 minutes for dariole moulds. Leave in the basin for a few minutes, then turn out.

COCOA-BEAN.

PRINCE ALBERT'S PUDDING

6 helpings

400g/13oz prunes
500ml/1 pint water
grated rind of 1 lemon
25g/1oz light soft brown sugar
butter for greasing

100g/4oz butter *or* margarine
100g/4oz caster sugar
2 eggs
40g/1½oz rice flour
100g/4oz brown breadcrumbs

SAUCE

1×5ml spoon/1 teaspoon arrowroot
250ml/½ pint prune liquid (see
  Method)

1×10ml spoon/1 dessertspoon
  granulated sugar
2–3 drops cochineal

Wash the prunes and soak them in the water overnight. Stew the prunes with half the lemon rind, the water and the brown sugar until soft. Strain and reserve 250ml/½ pint of the liquid for the sauce. Stone and halve the prunes. Line a buttered 1 litre/2 pint basin with the prunes, skin sides against the basin. Chop any prunes which are left over.

Cream together well the fat and caster sugar. Separate the eggs and beat the yolks into the creamed mixture. Add the remaining lemon rind, any chopped prunes, the rice flour, and the breadcrumbs. Whisk the egg whites until fairly stiff and fold into the mixture. Put into the basin, cover with greased paper or foil, and steam for 1½–1¾ hours.

Meanwhile, make the sauce. Blend the arrowroot to a smooth paste with some of the reserved prune liquid. Boil the rest of the liquid, and pour it gradually over the blended arrowroot, stirring all the time. Return to the saucepan, and bring to the boil, stirring all the time. Reduce the heat and simmer for 2–3 minutes. Add the sugar and cochineal.

When the pudding is cooked, leave for a few minutes, then turn out on to a serving dish and pour the sauce over it.

Prince Albert's Pudding

PATRIOTIC PUDDING

——————— *6 helpings* ———————

fat for greasing
3×15ml spoons/3 tablespoons red
   jam
200g/7oz plain flour
a pinch of salt
2×5ml spoons/2 teaspoons baking
   powder

100g/4oz butter *or* margarine
100g/4oz caster sugar
1 egg
75ml/3fl oz milk (approx)

Grease a 1 litre/2 pint basin and cover the bottom with the jam. Sift together the flour, salt, and baking powder. Rub the fat into the flour, salt and baking powder. Rub the fat into the flour and add the sugar. Beat the egg and milk together, and stir into the dry ingredients to form a soft dropping consistency. Put the mixture into the basin, cover with greased paper or foil, and steam for 1½–2 hours. Leave in the basin for a few minutes, then turn out.

    Serve with the same warmed jam as used in the recipe.

ALMOND PUDDINGS

——————— *4–8 helpings* ———————

fat for greasing
75g/3oz butter *or* margarine
75g/3oz caster sugar
3 eggs

150g/5oz ground almonds
3×15ml spoons/3 tablespoons
   single cream

Grease 8 dariole moulds. Cream together the fat and sugar. Separate the eggs and beat the yolks into the creamed mixture. Stir in the ground almonds and cream. Whisk the egg whites until as stiff as the main mixture, and fold them in lightly. Three-quarters fill the moulds, cover with greased paper or foil, and steam for 45–60 minutes until firm to the touch. Leave in the moulds for a few minutes, then turn out.

    Serve with warmed apricot or strawberry jam.

GUARDS PUDDING

100g/4oz butter *or* margarine
100g/4oz soft light *or* dark brown
  sugar
3×15ml spoons/3 tablespoons
  raspberry *or* strawberry jam
2 eggs
a pinch of salt

100g/4oz brown breadcrumbs
1×2.5ml spoon/½ teaspoon
  bicarbonate of soda
1×10ml spoon/1 dessertspoon
  warm water
butter for greasing

Cream together the fat and sugar, and beat in the jam. Mix in the
eggs, salt, and breadcrumbs. Dissolve the bicarbonate of soda in
the warm water and stir into the mixture. Put into a buttered 1
litre/2 pint basin, cover with greased paper or foil, and steam for 3
hours. Leave in the basin for a few minutes, then turn out.
    Serve with the same warmed jam as used in the recipe.

COCONUT PUDDING

150g/5oz plain flour
a pinch of salt
2×15ml spoons/2 teaspoons baking
  powder
50g/2oz butter *or* margarine

50g/2oz caster sugar
50g/2oz desiccated coconut
1 egg
50ml/2fl oz milk (approx)
fat for greasing

Sift together the flour, salt, and baking powder. Rub in the fat,
then add the sugar and coconut. Beat the egg and milk together,
stir into the dry ingredients, and mix to a soft dropping
consistency. Put the mixture into a greased 750ml/1½ pint basin,
cover with greased paper or foil and steam for 1½–2 hours. Leave
in the basin for a few minutes, then turn out.

BAKED PUDDINGS

JAM SPONGE PUDDING

4–6 helpings

100g/4oz butter *or* margarine
100g/4oz caster sugar
2 eggs
150g/5oz plain flour
1×5ml spoon/1 teaspoon baking
  powder

½×2.5ml spoon/¼ teaspoon
  vanilla essence
2×15ml spoons/2 tablespoons milk
  (approx)
2×15ml spoons/2 tablespoons jam
fat for greasing

Cream the fat and sugar together until light and fluffy. Beat the eggs until liquid, then beat them gradually into the creamed mixture. Sift together the flour and the baking powder, and fold them in. Add the essence and enough milk to form a soft dropping consistency. Put the jam in the bottom of a greased 1 litre/2 pint pie dish, then add the sponge mixture. Bake in a moderate oven at 180°C/350°F/Gas 4, for 30–35 minutes until well risen and golden-brown.

Serve from the dish with the same warmed jam as used in the recipe.

Note The pie dish can be encircled with a pie frill before presenting at table.

Jam Sponge Pudding

DEVONSHIRE RUM

—— *3–4 helpings* ——

250g/8oz (approx) cold Christmas
   pudding *or* rich fruit cake
fat for greasing
1 egg
2 × 10ml spoons/2 dessertspoons
   cornflour

250ml/½ pint milk
1 × 10ml spoon/1 dessertspoon soft
   brown sugar
50ml/2fl oz rum *or* a few drops rum
   essence

Cut the pudding or cake into fingers, and arrange in a greased
750ml/1½ pint pie dish. Beat the egg until liquid. Mix the
cornflour to a paste with a little of the milk. Heat the remaining
milk to scalding point, then pour it slowly on to the cornflour,
stirring to prevent lumps forming. Return it to the heat and cook
gently for 2 minutes; then stir in the sugar, egg, and rum or rum
essence. Pour the mixture over the pudding or cake and bake in a
moderate oven at 180°C/350°F/Gas 4, for about 30 minutes or until
firm.

EXETER PUDDING

5–6 helpings

butter for greasing
125g/5oz stale white breadcrumbs
25g/1oz ratafias *or* small macaroons
75g/3oz shredded suet
50g/2oz sago
75g/3oz caster sugar
grated rind and juice of 1 lemon

3 eggs
2×15ml spoons/2 tablespoons milk
25ml/1fl oz rum *or* to taste
(optional)
2 individual sponge cakes
75g/3oz jam (any type)

Butter a 1 litre/2 pint pie dish. Coat with some of the crumbs, and cover the bottom with half the ratafias or macaroons. Mix together the remaining crumbs, suet, sago, sugar, lemon rind, and juice. Beat together the eggs, milk, and rum, if used, and stir into the dry ingredients. Slice the sponge cakes. Put some of the mixture into the dish, cover with slices of sponge cake, a layer of jam, and some of the remaining ratafias. Repeat the layers until all the ingredients are used, finishing with a layer of breadcrumb mixture. Bake in a moderate oven at 180°C/350°F/Gas 4, for 45–60 minutes.

Serve with the same warmed jam as used in the recipe.

Overleaf
From the left
*Plums with Port (page 53), Eve's Pudding (page 49) and
Mrs Beeton's Bachelor's Pudding (page 36)*

COTTAGE PUDDING

5–6 helpings

200g/7oz plain flour
a pinch of salt
2×5ml spoons/2 teaspoons baking
  powder
100g/4oz butter *or* margarine

75g/3oz soft light brown sugar
100g/4oz raisins
1 egg
50–75ml/2–3fl oz milk
butter for greasing

Sift together the flour, salt, and baking powder. Rub the fat into the flour and add the rest of the dry ingredients. Beat the egg until liquid and stir into the dry ingredients with enough milk to make a soft dropping consistency. Put the mixture into a greased 25×20cm/10×8 inch baking dish and bake in a fairly hot oven at 190°C/375°F/Gas 5, for 35–40 minutes until firm in the centre and golden-brown.

Serve with Pouring Custard (page 17) or any sweet sauce

CASTLE PUDDINGS

3–4 helpings

100g/4oz butter *or* margarine
100g/4oz sugar
2 eggs
½×2.5ml spoon/¼ teaspoon
  vanilla essence

100g/4oz plain flour
1×5ml spoon/1 teaspoon baking
  powder
fat for greasing

Work together the fat and sugar until light and creamy. Beat in the eggs and vanilla essence. Sift together the flour and baking powder, and fold in the creamed mixture. Three-quarters fill 6–8 greased dariole moulds. Bake in a moderate oven at 180°C/350°F/Gas 4, for 20–25 minutes, until set and well risen.

Serve with Pouring Custard (page 17).

EVE'S PUDDING

4 helpings

400g/13oz cooking apples
grated rind and juice of 1 lemon
75g/3oz Demerara sugar
1 × 15ml spoon/1 tablespoon water
fat for greasing

75g/3oz butter *or* margarine
75g/3oz caster sugar
1 egg
100g/4oz self-raising flour

Peel, core, and slice the apples thinly. Mix together with the lemon rind and juice, Demerara sugar and water, and put into a greased 1 litre/2 pint pie dish. Cream the fat and caster sugar together until light and fluffy. Beat the egg until liquid and beat into the creamed mixture over the apples. Bake in a moderate oven at 180°C/350°F/Gas 4, for 40–45 minutes until the apples are soft and the sponge is firm

Serve with Pouring Custard (page 17) or melted apple jelly and single cream.

APPLE CRUMBLE

6 helpings

625g/1¼lb cooking apples
100g/4oz brown sugar
50ml/2fl oz water
grated rind of 1 lemon
fat for greasing

75g/3oz butter *or* margarine
150g/5oz plain flour
75g/3oz caster sugar
½ × 2.5ml spoon/¼ teaspoon
    ground ginger

Peel, core, and slice the apples. Cook with the brown sugar, water, and lemon rind in a covered pan until soft. Fill a greased 1 litre/2 pint pie dish with the apples. Rub the fat into the flour until it resembles fine breadcrumbs. Add the caster sugar and ginger and stir well, sprinkle the mixture over the apples, and press down lightly. Bake in a moderate oven at 180°C/350°F/Gas 4, for 30–40 minutes until the crumble is golden-brown.

ALMOND CASTLES

75g/3oz butter
75g/3oz caster sugar
3 eggs
3×15ml spoons/3 tablespoons
 single cream *or* milk

1×15ml spoon/1 tablespoon
 brandy (optional)
150g/5oz ground almonds
fat for greasing

Cream together the butter and sugar until light and fluffy.
Separate the eggs. Stir the egg yolk, cream or milk, brandy if used,
and ground almonds into the creamed mixture. Whisk the egg
whites until just stiff, and fold lightly into the mixture.
Three-quarters fill 8 greased dariole moulds. Bake in a warm oven
at 160°C/325°F/Gas 3, for 20–25 minutes, until the puddings are
firm in the centre and golden-brown.

Turn out and serve with Pouring Custard (page 17).

Almond Castles

FRUIT PUDDINGS

GOOSEBERRY FRITTERS

4 helpings

400g/13oz gooseberries
oil *or* fat for deep frying

caster sugar

BATTER

50g/2oz plain flour
a pinch of salt
1×15ml spoon/1 tablespoon caster
sugar

2 eggs
3×15ml spoons/3 tablespoons milk

Prepare the batter first. Sift together the flour and salt. Add the sugar. Separate the eggs. Mix the yolks and milk into the flour and beat well to form a thick batter. Prepare and dry the gooseberries. Heat the fat to 180–185°C/356–365°F. Whisk the egg whites until stiff and fold into the batter. Add the gooseberries. Dip a metal spoon in the hot fat, and then lift 3 coated gooseberries on to it. Lower them into the hot fat, without separating them. As the batter cooks, the berries will fuse together. Fry until golden-brown, turning once. Drain well.

Serve sprinkled with plenty of sugar.

GOOSEBERRY.